Python/Pitón

By Daisy Allyn   **Tradución al español: Nathalie Beullens**

 **Gareth Stevens** Publishing

Please visit our Web site, www.garethstevens.com. For a free color catalog of all our high-quality books, call toll free 1-800-542-2595 or fax 1-877-542-2596.

Cataloging Data

Allyn, Daisy.
Python / Pitón
    p. cm. — (Killer snakes / Serpientes asesinas)
Includes index.
ISBN 978-1-4339-4563-2 (library binding)
1. Pythons—Juvenile literature. I. Title.
QL666.O67A45 2011
597.96'78—dc22

                                    2010030693

First Edition

Published in 2011 by
Gareth Stevens Publishing
111 East 14th Street, Suite 349
New York, NY 10003

Copyright © 2011 Gareth Stevens Publishing

Designer: Michael J. Flynn
Editor: Greg Roza
Spanish translation: Nathalie Beullens

Photo credits: Cover, pp. 1, (2–4, 6–8, 10, 12, 14, 16, 18, 20–24 snake skin texture), 4–5, 6–7, 13, 17, 19, 21 Shutterstock.com; p. 9 iStockphoto.com; p. 11 Oxford Scientific/Photolibrary/Getty Images; p. 15 Werner Bollmann/Photolibrary/Getty Images.

Printed in the United States of America

CPSIA compliance information: Batch #CW11GS: For further information contact Gareth Stevens, New York, New York at 1-800-542-2595.

Contents

Contenido

Boldface words appear in the glossary/
Las palabras en **negrita** aparecen en el glosario

Big Snakes!

Pythons are large, strong snakes. There are 28 kinds of pythons in the world. They live in hot areas in Asia, Africa, and Australia. Pythons are good swimmers. They can also climb trees. Pythons kill by **squeezing** their **prey**!

- -

¡Serpientes gigantes!

Las pitones son serpientes grandes y fuertes. Existen 28 variedades de pitones en el mundo. Viven en las zonas cálidas de Asia, África y Australia. Las pitones son buenas nadadoras y también se trepan a los árboles. ¡Las pitones matan a sus **presas** con un **apretón**!

5

The Longest Snake

The reticulated (rih-TIH-kyuh-lay-tuhd) python is the longest snake in the world. It can be more than 30 feet (9.1 m) long and weigh 350 pounds (159 kg)! The reticulated python gets its name from the **patterns** on its skin. Something that is reticulated has criss-crossed lines.

La serpiente más larga

La pitón reticulada es la serpiente más larga del mundo. ¡Puede medir más de 30 pies (9.1 m) de largo, y pesar 350 libras (159 kg)! La pitón reticulada se llama así por el **diseño** de su piel. Algo que es reticulado tiene líneas entrecruzadas.

7

Python Babies

Female reticulated pythons lay eggs. A large reticulated python may lay up to 100 eggs at one time. After the female lays the eggs, she **coils** around them to keep them warm. Baby snakes break out of the eggs in about 85 days.

Pitones bebé

Las pitones reticuladas hembra ponen huevos. Una pitón reticulada grande puede poner hasta 100 huevos en una sola vez. Después de que los pone, se **enrosca** sobre ellos para mantenerlos calientes. Los pitones bebé salen del huevo en aproximadamente 85 días.

Once the baby reticulated pythons break out of their eggs, the mother leaves them. Each snake is about 30 inches (76 cm) long. Their colors help them hide from enemies such as hawks and cobras. Baby reticulated pythons eat mice, rats, lizards, and frogs.

Cuando los bebés de pitón reticulada salen del huevo, la madre los abandona. Cada serpiente mide aproximadamente 30 pulgadas (76 cm) de largo. Su color los ayuda a esconderse de sus enemigos, como por ejemplo, de los halcones y las cobras. Los bebés de pitón reticulada comen ratones, ratas, lagartijas y ranas.

11

Made for Hunting

Pythons are good hunters. They can see and smell very well. They use their tongues to smell. Pythons also have special parts on their faces called pits. Pits help pythons feel the heat of passing prey.

- -

Lista para cazar

Las pitones son buenas cazadoras. Tienen muy buena vista y olfato. Usan su lengua para sentir. Las pitones también tienen partes especiales en su cara que se llaman fosas. Las fosas ayudan a las pitones a sentir el calor de la presa que pase cerca.

13

The prey a python hunts depends on the python's size. Smaller pythons eat small animals, such as frogs and lizards. Reticulated pythons eat birds and rats. However, sometimes they eat larger animals, such as pigs and deer!

La presa que caza una pitón depende de su propio tamaño. Las pitones más pequeñas comen animales pequeños, como ranas y lagartijas. Las pitones reticuladas comen pájaros y ratas. Sin embargo, ¡algunas comen animales más grandes como cerdos y venados!

Python Teeth

Just like most snakes, pythons have two sharp teeth called fangs. However, pythons don't use their teeth to kill. Python teeth are hooked. The shape of a python's teeth helps the snake hold on to its prey.

Dientes de pitón

Como la mayor parte de las serpientes, las pitones tienen dos colmillos afilados, sin embargo las pitones no usan los colmillos para matar. Los dientes de pitón tienen forma de gancho. La forma de sus dientes le permite a la pitón sujetar su presa.

17

Sneaky Snake

A python often hides and waits for prey to go by. The python bites the prey and holds on. It quickly wraps its long body around the animal. Then it squeezes so hard the animal can't breathe. After the animal has died, the python swallows it in one gulp!

Serpiente sigilosa

A menudo, la pitón se esconde y espera a que pase su presa. La pitón muerde a su presa y la sujeta. Rápidamente envuelve al animal con su largo cuerpo y lo aprieta tan fuerte que el animal ya no puede respirar. Una vez el animal muerto, ¡la pitón se lo traga de un golpe!

19

Pythons and People

Pythons don't often **attack** people. In some places, pythons are used to kill pests, such as rats. Some people like to keep pythons as pets! Other people like to wear belts, boots, and coats made of python skin.

- -

Las pitones y la gente

Las pitones no **atacan** a menudo a la gente. En algunos lugares las pitones se usan para deshacerse de plagas, como las ratas. ¡Hay gente a quien le gusta tener pitones como mascotas! Otros usan la piel de pitón en cinturones, botas y abrigos.

Snake Facts/
Hoja informativa

Reticulated Python/
Pitón reticulada

Length/ Longitud	some can be more than 30 feet (9.1 m) long algunas pueden medir más de 30 pies (9.1 m) de largo
Weight/Peso	up to 350 pounds (159 kg) hasta 350 libras (159 kg)
Where It Lives/ Hábitat	Africa, Asia, Australia; hot places África, Asia, Australia; zónas cálidas
Life Span/ Años de vida	25 to 30 years de 25 a 30 años
Killer Fact/ Datos mortales	The longest snake ever recorded was a reticulated python found in Indonesia in 1902. It was nearly 33 feet (10 m) long! La serpiente más larga, fue una pitón reticulada encontrada en Indonesia en 1902. ¡Medía casi 33 pies (10 m) de largo!

Glossary/Glosario

attack: to try to harm someone or something

coil: to wrap around something many times

pattern: the way colors or shapes happen over and over again

prey: an animal hunted by other animals for food

squeeze: to press something tightly

- -

apretón (el) apretar algo muy fuerte

atacar tratar de dañar a alguien o a algo

diseño (el) la manera en que los colores o las formas se repiten

enroscar envolver algo muchas veces

presa (la) un animal cazado por otro animal para comérselo

For More Information/Más información

Books/Libros

Goldish, Meish. *Reticulated Python: The World's Longest Snake.* New York, NY: Bearport Publishing, 2010.

Gunderson, Megan M. *Pythons.* Edina, MN: ABDO Publishing, 2011.

Web Sites/Páginas en Internet

Reptiles: Python

www.sandiegozoo.org/animalbytes/t-python.html
Read about pythons and find out how they are different from other snakes.

Reticulated Pythons

animal.discovery.com/fansites/crochunter/australiazoo/40reticpython.html
Learn more about the reticulated python.

Index/Índice